THE MYTHICAL DETECTIVE
LOKI RAGNAROK
1
Sakura Kinoshita

Contents

URD, WHY DIDN'T YOU...

FORCE MASTER LOKI TO COME BACK TO THE WORLD OF THE GODS?

PERHAPS WE COULD HAVE STOPPED LORD ODIN THEN... BUT WE CAN NO LONGER CONTROL DESTINY.

THE TIME OF RAGNAROK IS APPROACHING...

IT'LL BE **FUN**.

CHAPTER 1
The End of the World

huff
huff
There's still time...
We won't let them have their way.
CREAK
So they're finally here...

But YOU must do something for me...

I am the MYTHICAL DETECTIVE... Don't forget!
They call me the Mythical Detective... Loki!
I will solve...
any case to your satisfaction!
(not completely true)
PMEOW
IT'S A RADIO WAVE!
WAAUGH
GYAAA

YOU'RE IN A GOOD MOOD, DAD. YOU'RE EVEN SINGING. ♡
I'LL GIVE YOU ONE, TOO, FENRIR.
WHY HAS EVERYONE FALLEN DOWN?
I STOOD IN LINE FOR AN **HOUR** TO BUY THESE. THEY'RE GONNA BE SO GOOD!
......
SMILE
I CAME HERE FROM THE WORLD OF THE GODS TO SEE YOU, DAD...
I WAS **SO** SURPRISED TO FIND YOU IN THE FORM OF A CHILD.
IT'S LIKE YOU'VE BECOME A CHILD BOTH INSIDE AND OUT. YOU'RE NOTHING LIKE THE MIGHTY **TRICKSTER** YOU USED TO BE, DAD!
DON'T YOU KNOW WHAT **IMAGAWAYAKI** ARE, ETCHAN? SOMETIMES THEY'RE CALLED KAITENYAKI, OBANYAKI, TAIKOYAKI OR SIMPLY OYAKI.
憧れてたのに……
I USED TO REVERE YOU...
BO
BOOKS
Sale

THD
SOME SAY A BAKER STARTED SELLING THEM AT THE END OF EDO ERA, NEAR IMAGAWA BRIDGE IN KANDA DISTRICT IN TOKYO.
THD
THD
FAMOUS IMAGAWAYAKI
HEY, YOU CAN'T JUST EAT AND RUN! STOP RIGHT THERE!!
!
KA-THUD!
WH-
WHAT'S THE MATTER?!
MISS...

WELL...
STARE
IMAGAWA-YAKI?

GRAB
DASH
YEAAARGH!!
WHERE DID THAT DINE-AND-DASH GIRL GO?
WHAT DO YOU THINK YOU'RE DOING?!
DAMN!
BY ANY CHANCE ...
ちらり。
GLANCE

THAT'S MY...

I...

IMAGAWAYA...

munch
munch
MASTER LOKI. IT'S HOPELESS.
ALL THAT YOUNG LADY DOES IS EAT. SHE DOESN'T TALK AT ALL.
......
MUNCH
MUNCH
ぶすぅ
SIGH

HUH?
SHE ATE THEM ALL...
MUMBLE
NEVER MIND. I'M JUST TALKING TO MYSELF. SO YAMINO, YOU DON'T KNOW HER NAME OR WHERE SHE CAME FROM, THEN?
RIGHT. IF YOU ASK HER NAME, ALL SHE DOES IS SHAKE HER HEAD.
MAYBE...
SHE HAS...
AMNESIA.
WHY THE HECK DID I END UP WITH HER?! I GUESS I HAVE TO CALL THE POLICE.
YAMINO, COULD YOU CALL MASUMI?
ちょこん
FWSH
WHOA! YOU SNEAKED UP ON ME!

SOB
SHAKE
SHAKE
MUNCH
MUNCH
GULP
GARGH!!
IF YOU HAVE SOMETHING TO SAY, THEN SPIT IT OUT!
EAT OR SPEAK! ONE OR THE OTHER!
MASTER LOKI,
I THINK SHE WISHES TO STAY HERE.
HUFF HUFF
N... NO WAY.
NOD
NOD
NOD

SHE'S NOT SAYING ANYTHING.
MAYBE SHE **CAN'T** TALK.
CAN'T TALK?
......
I UNDER-STAND.

I'LL LET HER STAY UNTIL SHE GETS HER MEMORY BACK.
I'M SO GLAD.
HOWEVER...
THIS IS A DETECTIVE AGENCY. YOU WILL HELP ME WITH MY DETECTIVE WORK.
AND YOU'LL HELP YAMINO, TOO. THOSE ARE MY ORDERS!
MUNCH
MUNCH
はぐ はぐ はぐ
MUNCH
ARE YOU LISTENING?
MASTER LOKI?
LOKI

WE NEED A NAME FOR HER. WHAT WOULD YOU LIKE TO CALL HER?
LET'S SEE...
WE'LL CALL HER SPICA.
SPICA?
VIRGO IS KNOWN AS A GODDESS HOLDING SHEAVES OF WHEAT.
THE BRIGHTEST STAR LOCATED AT THE SPIKE OF THE WHEAT IS SPICA.
DON'T BE A GOOD-FOR-NOTHING, OKAY?

SWP
WELL, THAT'S IT FOR EATING.
GO DO YOUR CHORES, SPICA.
UNTIL YOU GET YOUR MEMORY BACK, THAT'S YOUR NAME.
I AM THE MASTER OF THIS HOUSEHOLD. UNDER-STOOD?
......
NOW THEN, SPICA. LET'S GET SOME CLEANING DONE.

FIRST, LET'S CHANGE INTO SOME WORK CLOTHES.
YAMINO, YOU REALLY LIKE SPICA, DON'T YOU?
MAYBE SO.
I WONDER WHY.
MASTER LOKI, IF YOU WANT ME TO KICK HER OUT, I'LL DO AS YOU SAY.
NO. I WOULDN'T DO THAT.
YES. I KNOW.
K-CHK
I WONDER WHY...

WOW!
YOU LOOK VERY NICE, SPICA.
WHERE DID YOU FIND THAT MAID'S UNIFORM?
I PUT WHAT WE HAD TOGETHER.
PUT IT TOGETHER?
THUD

AAAAH!
MY CHAIR!!
OH DEAR! OH DEAR!
オロオロオロオ
MAYBE SPICA IS...
A SUPER KLUTZY GIRL.
NOW THEN.
I'M GOING TO BED.
YAMINO WILL SHOW YOU THE REST.

SPICA, YOU DID MOST OF THE **EATING**. SO CLEAN UP THE KITCHEN BEFORE GOING TO B...
......
FENRIR SEEMS TO BE ATTACHED TO SPICA ALREADY.
PMEOW-MEOW IS ATTACHED TO HER, TOO. SHE DOESN'T SEEM STRANGE TO ME, EITHER.
HMM...
GOOD NIGHT, SPICA.

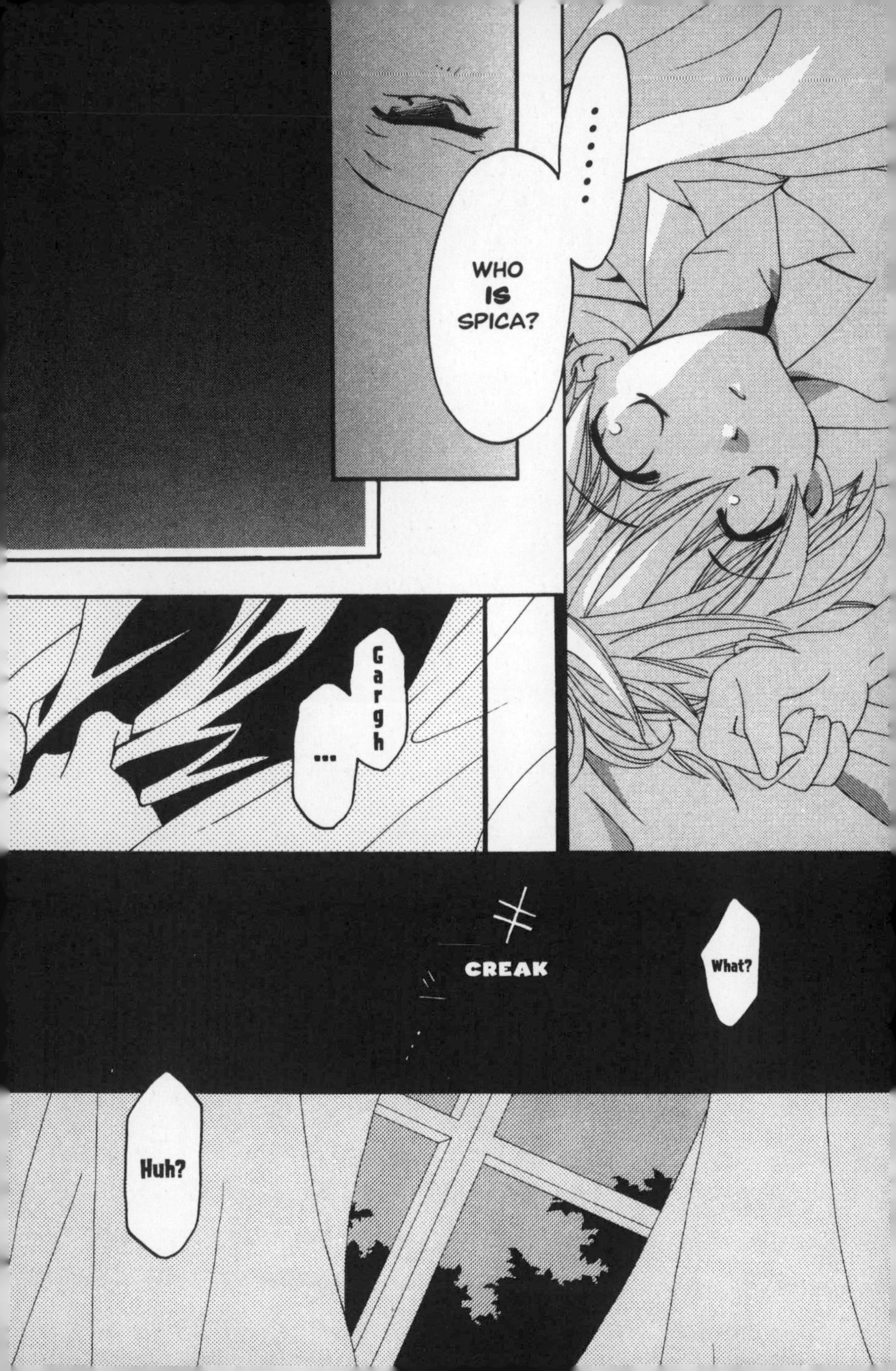

....
WHO IS SPICA?
Gargh...
CREAK
What?
Huh?

S...
Spica.

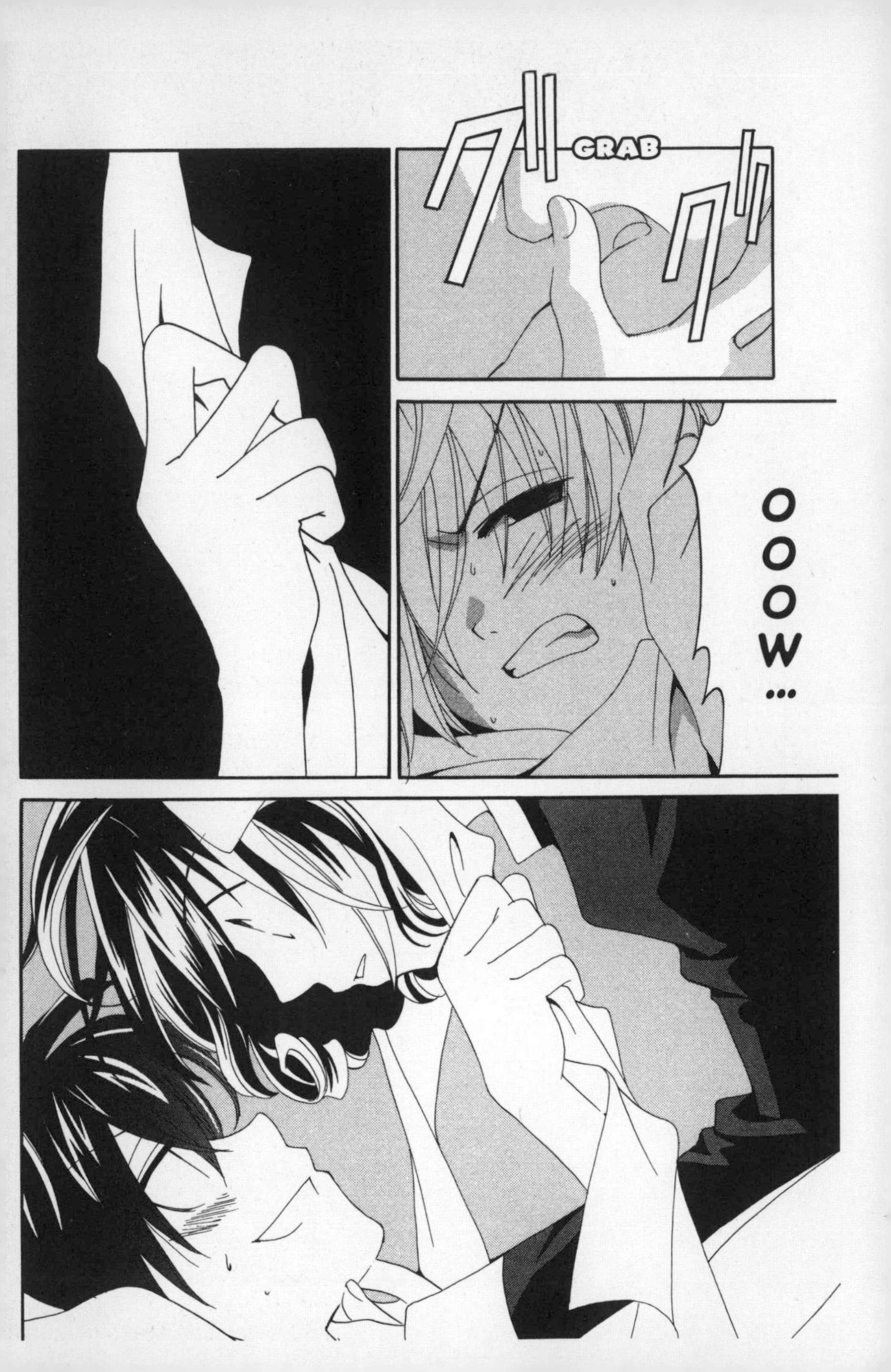
GRAB
OOOW...

KONK
MASTER LOKI, WHAT WAS THAT SOUND?!
PSHOOO
SPICA TRIED TO STRANGLE ME...
WHAT?!

DID MASTER LOKI GIVE YOU A HEAD-BUTT? SPICA, YOU POOR BABY.
HEY, IS **SHE** MORE IMPORTANT TO YOU THAN ME?
FSHOOM
WAIT!
I'M KIDDING.
FOR SURE.
DOES THIS MEAN SPICA IS AFTER YOUR LIFE?
I CAN'T BELIEVE THAT...
MASTER LOKI?

OH, NO!!

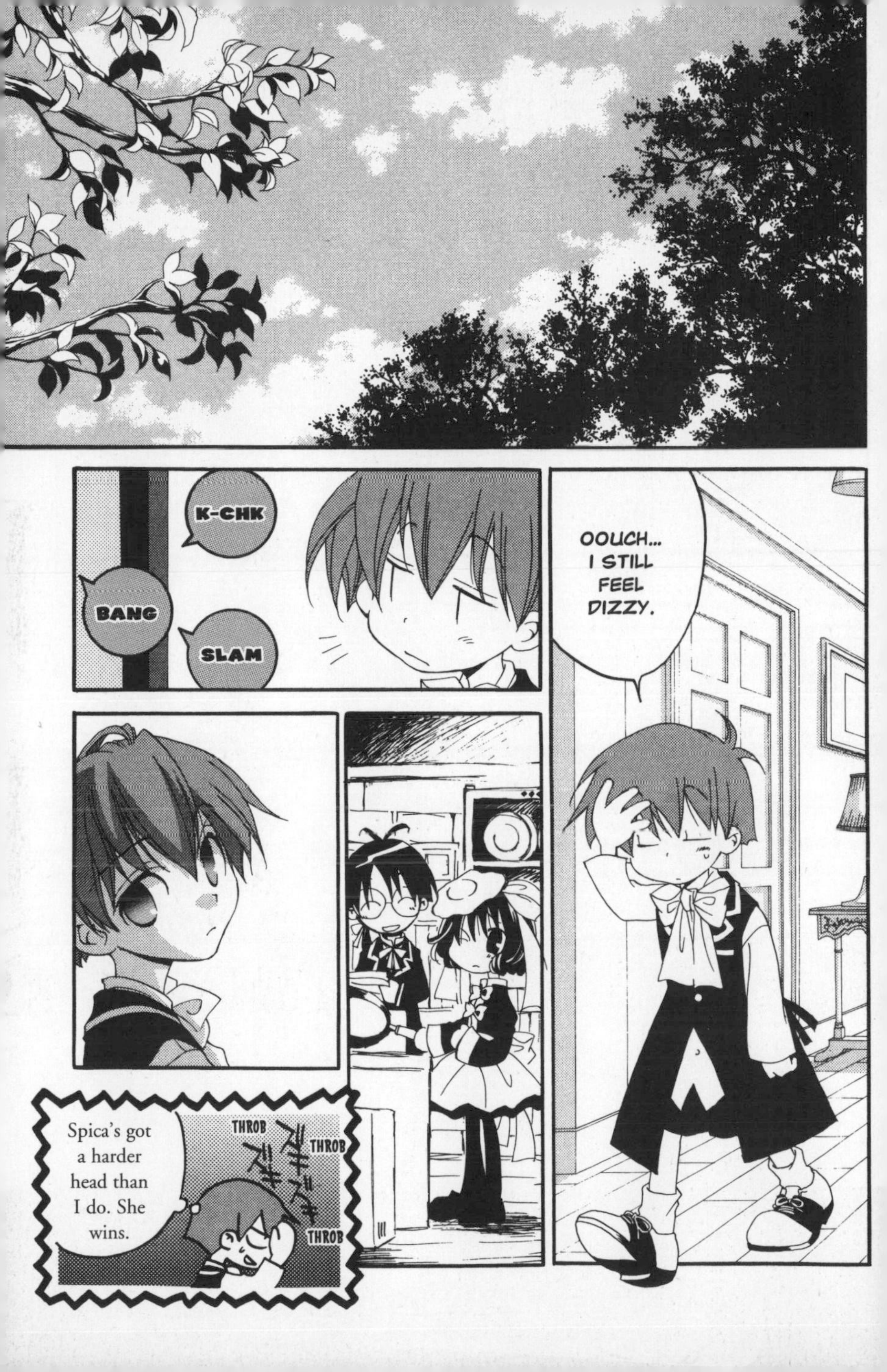
OOUCH... I STILL FEEL DIZZY.
K-CHK
BANG
SLAM
Spica's got a harder head than I do. She wins.
THROB
THROB
THROB

GOOD MORNING, YAMINO.
FWSH
MASTER LOKI, YOU'RE AWAKE!
SPICA DOESN'T REMEMBER ANYTHING ABOUT LAST NIGHT.
I SEE.
......
NOW THAT YOU'RE AWAKE, ARE YOU READY FOR BREAKFAST?
......
LET'S JUST KEEP AN EYE ON HER FOR A WHILE.

MUNCH
MUNCH
MUNCH
MUNCH
SHE SURE CAN EAT THOUGH.
NIBBLE
NIBBLE
LAST NIGHT, SPICA CLEANED UP THE STOVE SPICK AND SPAN.
TIMER
......
SHE WORKED ON IT EVEN AFTER I WENT TO BED. SHE WANTED TO MAKE IT SPARKLING CLEAN.

IT'S GOING TO BE ANOTHER SLOW DAY.
......
SPICA IS TRYING TO KILL ME... IS SHE AN ASSASSIN SENT BY ODIN?
WHO IS SPICA?
IT FEELS LIKE I KNOW HER...
HMM
MUNCH
MUNCH
SIGH
HELLO! MASTER LOKI!

I BROUGHT YOU SOME VEGETABLES I GREW IN MY GARDEN, MASTER LOKI!
WOW. YOU GREW THEM, REYA?
THEY ARE SOOO DELICIOUS!
I GAVE THEM LOTS AND LOTS OF WATER, SO THEY'D GET NICE AND BIG.
I WANTED TO MAKE YOU HAPPY, MASTER LOKI.

THANK YOU!
......
I'VE BEEN HAVING STRANGE DREAMS THESE DAYS.
WHAT?

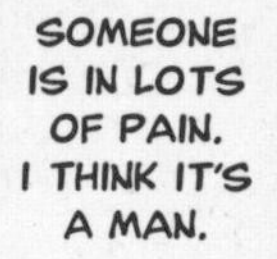

SOMEONE IS IN LOTS OF PAIN. I THINK IT'S A MAN.

HE WANTS THE PAIN TO GO AWAY, BUT HE HAS TO HURT MASTER LOKI FOR IT TO STOP.

IS YOUR DREAM A PROPHECY, REYA?
WHY DO I HAVE SUCH BAD DREAMS?
CLINK CLINK
SPICA, BE CAREFUL.
TOTTER

K-SHANG
......
WHO IS SHE, MASTER LOKI?
SHE STARTED WORKING HERE AS OF TODAY. RIGHT, SPICA?
FLAP FLAP
ぱたぱた

CRUNCH
CRUNCH
CRUNCH
CRUNCH
CRUNCH
CABBAGE
REYA, WHAT ELSE CAN YOU TELL ME ABOUT THE MAN?
WELL...
CRUNCH
CRUNCH
DON'T WORRY ABOUT SPICA. JUST IGNORE HER.
MY PRECIOUS VEGETABLES ARE DISAPPEARING.

I GREW THEM FOR YOU, MASTER LOKI.
I WORKED SO HARD TO GROW MY VEGETABLES.
REYA!
DASH
THAT'S SOOO MEAN!
WAAA
WAAA
WAAA
WAAA
YO, LOKI!!
HELLO, EVERYONE. ARE YOU BEHAVING YOURSELVES?
YOO-HOO

THUD
REYA JUST RAN PAST ME, CRYING. WHAT THE HECK DID YOU DO?
Like peas in a pod
HUH?
CRUNCH
CRUNCH
I SEE. YOU DID IT AGAIN.
WHAT ARE YOU TALKING ABOUT, NARUKAMI?!
MMN
THIS IS SPICA. SHE STARTED WORKING HERE TODAY.
MMN

I HOPE REYA DOESN'T TURN INTO FREYA...
YOU KNOW WHAT, NARUKAMI? SHE HAD A DREAM!
SO?! I HAD A DREAM I GOT A LETTER FROM A PANDA. SHE SAID SHE WAS WAITING FOR ME IN THE WATER.
THEN SHE TURNED INTO JELLO.
NOT THAT KIND OF STUPID DREAM.
REYA IS THE INCARNATION OF FREYA. CAN WHAT SHE DREAMS...
BE A PROPHECY?
SOMEONE WHO WISHES TO KILL ME... MOST LIKELY IT'S ODIN.
BECAUSE OF THE PAIN HE IS IN, HE WANTS TO KILL ME.
HE'S IN PAIN? IS HE ILL?
I COULD SEE MYSELF GETTING SICK AS A HUMAN, BUT I'VE NEVER HEARD OF A GOD GETTING SICK.
IF HE CAN'T COME KILL ME HIMSELF, WHAT WOULD HE DO?

WHY DOES HIS ILLNESS HAVE ANYTHING TO DO WITH YOU?
MAYBE IT'S...
BECAUSE THE GODS AND I HAVE A CERTAIN RELATIONSHIP WITH THE GIANTS.
SNIFF
SNIFF
SNIFF
OH, I BROUGHT SOME OKONOMIYAKI. I WORK PART-TIME AT THIS SHOP.
AS USUAL, YOU LACK DIGNITY AS A GOD, NARUKAMI.
SNUGGLE
SPICA, GO AHEAD AND HAVE SOME.
HEY, NARUKAMI, WHAT IS ODIN...?
OH!
YOO-HOO!
SOMEONE'S HERE.

HI LOKI! HAVE YOU GOTTEN ANY COOL CASES YET?
UH-OH, IT'S THE NOISIEST ONE OF ALL.
SHE'S SO LOUD.
YO!
DAIDOJI. LONG TIME NO SEE.
HUH? WE SAW EACH OTHER AT SCHOOL, NARUGAMI.
OOPS! I'M GONNA BE LATE FOR WORK!!
FWUMP

HUH? I DIDN'T KNOW YOU WORE A WATCH.
I DO.
I'M ALWAYS BUSY, YOU KNOW. I DREW A WATCH HERE (WITH PERMANENT MARKER).
SO I WON'T FORGET THINGS.
SEE YA!
EXIT
ARE YOU REALLY THOR?
HEY, LOKI.
A CASE? I HAVEN'T SEEN ANY COOL CASES TODAY.
THAT'S NOT WHAT I MEAN.
WHO IS THIS GIRL?
MUNCH
MUNCH
MUNCH
YOU COULD CALL HER A "COOL" CASE...

I SEE. SPICA HAS AMNESIA AND CAN'T SPEAK.
THAT MUST BE DIFFICULT.
I'M DETECTIVE LOKI'S ASSISTANT, MAYURA DAIDOJI.
LET ME KNOW IF I CAN BE OF ANY HELP.
LOKI IS COLD-HEARTED.
I AM?
I GOT SOME OF THOSE PASTRIES EVERYBODY'S TALKING ABOUT.
SQUEAK
SQUEAK
SQUEAK
HEY, SPICA! WHY ARE YOU SO HUNGRY? POOR BABY.
YOU'RE ACTING LIKE I **DON'T** FEED YOU.
MAYBE SPICA KNOWS YOU, LOKI.
BA-DUMP
WHAT?
REMEMBER THE STORY OF THE MERMAID PRINCESS WHO GAVE UP HER VOICE TO BE WITH THE PRINCE?

THE UNFULFILLED LOVE OF THE MERMAID PRINCESS.
REMEMBER, FREYR- DO NOT LET LOKI KNOW I'M BACK TO MY ORIGINAL FORM.
SCUFF
SCUFF
I KNOW, HEIMDAL.
SCUFF
HE'LL BE CAUGHT TOTALLY OFF-GUARD. HIS COWARDLY FACE WILL TWIST IN ANGUISH.
THE TIME HAS COME TO SETTLE THE SCORE, LOKI!!
HEH HEH HEH HEH...
BWA HA HA
AFTER EATING THESE SPECIAL BUNS.
KNOW NOTHIN'
Snacks

YOU NEVER LEARN, DO YOU? LOKI DEFEATED YOU SO BADLY, BUT YOU STILL DON'T GIVE UP.
I GUESS YOU **CAN'T** GO BACK, BECAUSE ODIN STRIPPED YOU OF YOUR GODHOOD.
WHAT'RE YOU TALKING ABOUT, FREYR?! **YOU** FAILED TO PUT LOKI UNDER THAT SPELL!
WHY DIDN'T YOU JUST GO BACK TO THE WORLD OF THE GODS?
I WILL STAY HERE FOR A WHILE.
WHY?
I NEVER EXPECTED SPICA TO EAT ALL OF THE PASTRIES.
I'M GONNA GO BUY MORE FOR LOKI.
NJAKU DETECTIVE AGENCY
MA-YU-RAAA!
まーゆーらーちゃーん
THAT WAS A STUPID QUESTION...

HELLO!
IT'S ME, KAZUMI HIGASHIYAMA!
WHISPER
WHISPER
MAN, I FEEL SO UNCOMFORTABLE HERE.
hello hello
H... Hello, Loki!
I came to visit you!
His voice is shaking.
Trying hard to smile.

HI, KAZUMI. HOW HAVE YOU BEEN? HOW NICE OF YOU TO COME VISIT!
REALLY? YOU'RE EMBARRASSING ME.
WHAT WAS THAT? DOES HE KNOW WHO I AM? IT CAN'T BE...
ALL I NEED IS FOR HIM TO EAT THESE BUNS. JUST DO IT!
LET'S GET IT ON!
SNACK BOX
I BROUGHT THESE DELICIOUS BUNS!
I WANTED YOU TO ENJOY THEM, LOKI.
MMM. SMELLS GOOD! NOW OPEN WIDE! ♡
ぱくっ
CHOMP
MUNCH
MUNCH
IS SHE ALRIGHT?
......
はっ
HUH!

IMPOSSIBLE!! IT CAN'T BE!
GREGHH!
It IS a super-hot bun made with whole chili peppers! How the heck can she eat it?!
BURP!
BWOOF
I WON'T FORGET THIS, LOKI.
EXIT
TOTTER
TOTTER
IT WOULD BE BETTER FOR YOU, IF I WERE TO FORGET ABOUT THIS.

...ALL THAT REMAINS OF THE SOLDIERS' DREAMS.
OH DEAR. SPICA CAN EAT A LOT, CAN'T SHE?
WHY DID THEY COME TO VISIT ME TODAY?
That's the question.
I'M TIRED.
MASTER LOKI, WHY DON'T YOU TAKE A REST?
YEAH.
I'LL TAKE A BREAK AND READ A BOOK.
SPICA AND I WILL CLEAN UP.

laundry
THUP
THUP
THUP
FWUMP
BUT SHE DOESN'T LOOK LIKE AN ASSASSIN.
I DON'T WANT TO THINK ABOUT IT.
WHAT IS MAKING HER THE WAY SHE IS...
TICK
TOCK
TICK
TOCK
TICK
TOCK
DOZING
DOZING
K-CHK
Don't be so stupid. "Kakkurakin" isn't on any more!
RUN, PLEASE!!
MASTER LOKI!!
AWAKE

SPICA...
STAB

THWOMP

NOW THEN...
LET'S PUT SPICA ON THE COUCH SO SHE CAN REST.

....
....
I WAS PICKING UP THE EMPTY BOX FROM MAYURA'S PASTRIES.
WHEN SPICA SAW ME, SHE GRABBED THE KITCHEN KNIFE.
THE COOKING RANGE... THE EMPTY BOX... WHAT IS GOING ON?
MASTER LOKI, WHAT ARE YOU GOING TO DO WITH SPICA?
I'M GOING BACK TO MY ROOM TO THINK ABOUT IT.
HI, LOKI!
I'M BACK FOR A RETURN MATCH! ♡
....

THMP
THMP
THAT'S SO THOUGHTFUL OF YOU, MAYURA.
I'LL PREPARE SOME TEA.
WHAT'S WRONG WITH SPICA?
PLEASE LEAVE HER ALONE. SHE'S TIRED.
OF COURSE SHE'S TIRED. SHE CAN'T TALK, SHE'S LOST HER MEMORY, AND YOU MAKE HER WORK.
DON'T PUT IT LIKE THAT, MAYURA.
ALL SPICA DOES IS HELP YAMINO.
ISN'T THAT BETTER THAN DYING IN A DITCH?
BESIDES, SHE EATS A **LOT**!
YAMINO, HAVE YOU NOTICED ANYTHING DIFFERENT ABOUT HER?
......
MAYURA, WHEN DO YOU THINK OF YOUR MOM?

WHAT?
WHAT KIND OF QUESTION IS THAT?
SMILE
LET ME SEE...
LIKE WHEN I SEE A TOY PANDA, OR AN AMUSEMENT PARK...
THOSE ARE HAPPY MEMORIES OF YOUR MOM.
THEY REMIND YOU OF THE GOOD TIMES YOU SPENT WITH HER.
YEAH. HOW DID YOU KNOW?
HOW MEMORY WORKS
INFO
Remember
Memory is registered in the brain.
Recollection
THE STRONGER THE EMOTIONS TIED TO EVENTS ARE,
THE EASIER IT IS FOR THE HUMAN BRAIN TO REGISTER THEM AS MEMORIES.
IT IS CALLED "EPISODIC MEMORY."

AND WHEN YOU MEMORIZE WORDS, THAT'S "SEMANTIC MEMORY."
DOES MAYURA HAVE IT...?
I SEE.
ふ〜ん
DOES THAT MEAN SPICA CAN'T READ OR WRITE BECAUSE SHE LOST HER MEMORY?
EPISODIC MEMORY AND SEMANTIC MEMORY ARE PROCESSED IN DIFFERENT PARTS OF THE BRAIN.
AMNESIACS LIKE SPICA OFTEN SUFFER DISORDERS IN EPISODIC MEMORY.
THE FACT THAT SHE CAN CARRY ON IN HER DAILY LIFE INDICATES...
HER SEMANTIC MEMORY IS ALL RIGHT.
OH!
I GET IT!!
びっくぅ!!
WINCE
WHAT? WHAT?!
DID I SAY SOMETHING BAD?!
FLASH
YAY!

MAYURA, LET ME SEE THE PASTRY BOX. IT'S THE SAME AS BEFORE, RIGHT?
YEAH. IT IS.
IF SPICA SAW AN ARROW ON THE COOKING STOVE...
SQRK
SQRK
ANSUR...
"ANSUR"?
HAVE YOU EVER HEARD OF RUNES?
AREN'T THEY ANCIENT LETTERS? AND EACH HAS A CURSE AND MAGICAL MEANING?
I THINK THEY USE THOSE FOR JEWELRY DESIGNS, TOO.
ANSUR MEANS MOUTH, IT ALSO MEANS...
ODI...

...UGH!!
SPICA!!
GAARGH!

WHAT THE HECK ARE YOU DOING, SPICA?!
Waaugh!
ガターン!
CLATTER
MAYURA! HELP ME!! JUST FOLLOW ME!
OKAY!
I HAVE NO IDEA WHAT'S GOING ON, BUT WE HAVE TO STOP SPICA!
ゴッ
BAM

WAVER
!
HUFF
HUFF

SPICA!!
SPICA'S VOICE WAS SEALED...
COUGH
HUH
BY ODIN'S CURSE.
COUGH
MASTER LOKI...
SPICA **DIDN'T** HAVE AMNESIA.
I WAS...
UMM ...
WHAT HAPPENED TO SPICA?

HM... WELL, MAYURA!
TELL ME HOW THE MERMAID PRINCESS GETS HER VOICE BACK!
GEEZ. WHY ARE YOU SO SHAKEN UP?
SHE COULDN'T EXPRESS HER LOVE TO THE PRINCE.
SHE GOT SO UPSET SHE FINALLY THREW HERSELF INTO THE OCEAN.

SPLOOSH

SHE RESCUED ME, INSTEAD OF ME RESCUING HER...
WHEEZE
WHEEZE
HUFF
HUFF
WHEEZE
WHEEZE
A HA HA
あはは…
laughing at himself
……
CHUCKLE
CHUCKLE
CHUCKLE
!

......
SPICA, YOUR VOICE...
AH...
THE CURSE IS LIFTED!!
WHY DID YOU COME HERE?
YOU EVEN WENT SO FAR AS TO GET CURSED.
I WANTED TO SEE YOU...
MUTTER

......
NO WONDER YAMINO AND FENRIR WERE SO ATTACHED TO YOU.
IT'S BECAUSE YOU ARE–
HUH?
YOU ...
YOU CAN KEEP CALLING ME SPICA.

HEY YAMINO! I'M GOING OUT FOR A WHILE. OH?
ARE YOU EATING AGAIN, SPICA?
......
GO AHEAD! EAT AS MUCH AS YOU LIKE!
FWSH...

SINCE SHE EATS SO MUCH,
I'D BETTER WORK HARDER... (A LIE)
TMP
TMP
MASTER LOKI, ARE YOU GOING OUT?
BY THE WAY,
DID YOU KNOW WHO SPICA WAS FROM THE BEGINNING?
OF COURSE! PARENTS AND CHILDREN SHARE A BOND OF BLOOD!
......

I WAS THE ONLY ONE WHO DIDN'T KNOW...
しょんぼり
DEJECTED
WATCH OUT, MASTER LOKI!!
LOKI! WHAT SPECIAL MYSTERY DO YOU HAVE TODAY?
KA-THUD
ドガーン
......

IT TURNED OUT NICE. SPICA CAN SPEAK NOW, AND SHE'S GOT HER MEMORY BACK.
MY EFFORTS HAVE PAID OFF.
I STILL HAVE A BUMP ON MY HEAD.
SO, LOKI. WHAT'S TODAY'S CASE ABOUT?
I'M GOING TO BUY SOME IMAGA-WAYAKI.
WHAT?

SHE'S SUCCESSFULLY ENTERED THEIR GROUP.
THE GIANTESS, SHE WHO BIRTHED THE THREE MONSTERS OF LOKI THE TRICKSTER.
ANGRBODA: THE "OMEN OF GRIEF."

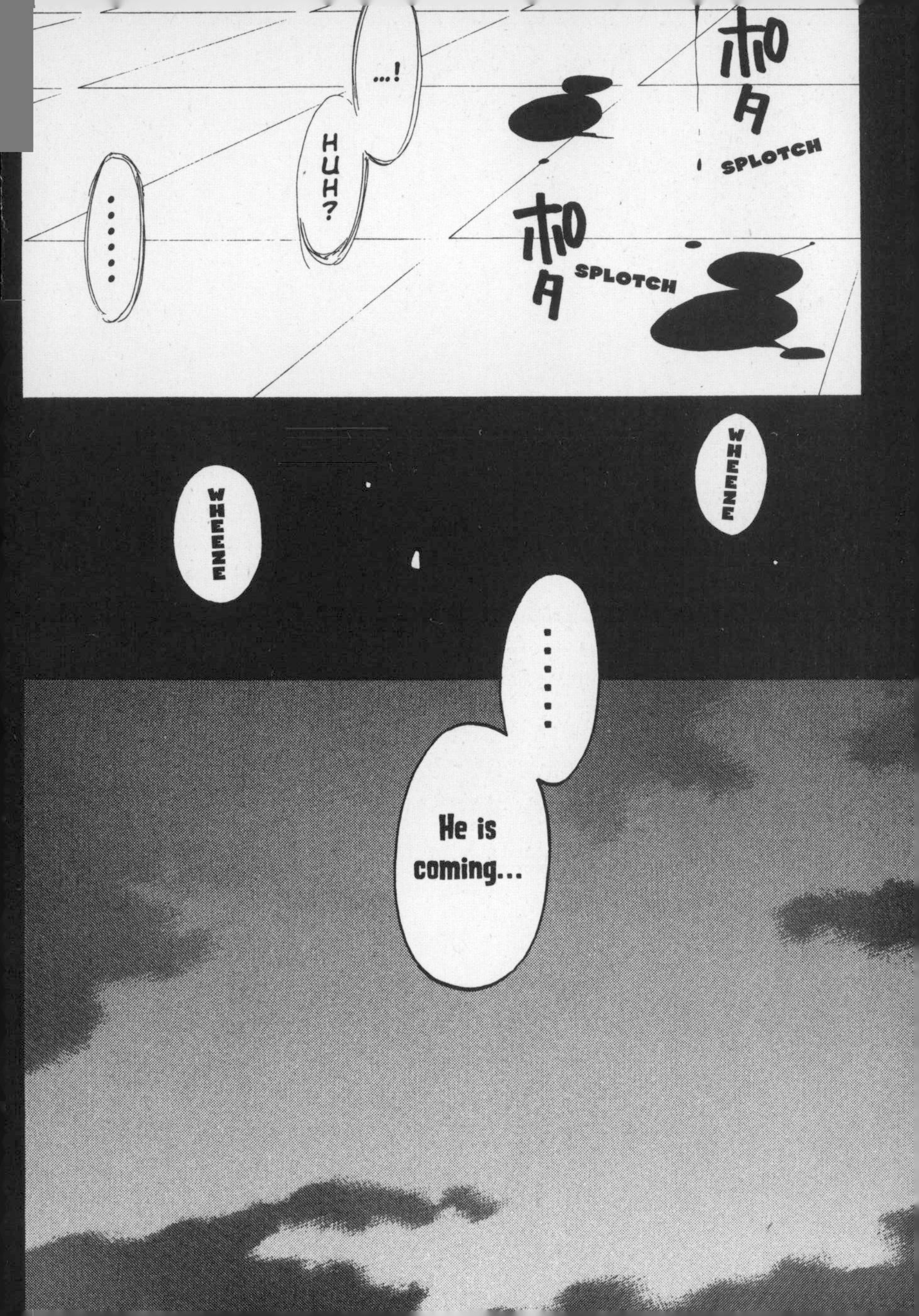
ポタ
SPLOTCH
ポタ
SPLOTCH
...!
HUH?
......
WHEEZE
WHEEZE
......
He is coming...

CHAPTER 2
The Taste of Milk

LOKI'S FAMILY GET-TOGETHER
......

HEY, DAIDOJI!
WAIT UP!
OH, NARUGAMI! WHAT ABOUT YOUR JOB?
I'M ONLY WORKING MORNINGS NOW.
SO I'M FREE AFTER SCHOOL, AND I THOUGHT I'D GO BUM MUNCHIES OFF OF LOKI. LET'S GO.
HE SAID TODAY'S SNACK WOULD BE FRESH DONUTS.
YEAH.
I'M NOT GOING TO BUM FOOD FROM LOKI THOUGH.
WHAT'S WRONG? YOU DON'T LOOK HAPPY AT ALL.
WE ARE BROTHERS, WE ARE FRIENDS, LET'S BE HAPPY TOGETHER ...
HUH?

THIS SONG IS MY PERSONAL MOTTO.
CLENCH
BUT ...
SPICA DOESN'T TALK TO ME!!
WHAT DID I DO TO MAKE HER MAD AT ME?
TOTALLY IGNORES ME!
HELLO
OOH!
SKIDDD
NEVER TALKS TO ME.
SHE'S THE QUIET TYPE.
PLEASE NARUGAMI, TELL ME HOW I CAN BECOME FRIENDS WITH SPICA.
NOT ESPECIALLY.
SHAKE
SHAKE
DON'T YOU FEEL ALIENATED WHEN YOU'RE WITH HER?
I KNOW VERY WELL THAT TALKING TO YOU WILL NOT HELP MATTERS ANY.
STUPID MAYURA!!
AAAA
DON'T WORRY, DAIDOJI.
REMEMBER, A MAN DIES ALONE.
WHAT KIND OF AN ANSWER IS THAT?

SPICA, DIDN'T YOU SEE ODIN BEFORE YOU CAME HERE?
DID YOU NOTICE ANYTHING DIFFERENT ABOUT HIM?
ANYTHING?
LIKE, WAS HE IN PAIN...?
HMM.
I SEE.
......

ARE YOU THIRSTY, SPICA?
GO BUY SOMETHING TO DRINK.
HE SENT ASSASSINS MANY TIMES.
YET, SOMEHOW I HAVE A SENSE OF TRUST IN ODIN.
IT'S ABSURD ...
OH, IT'S LOKI. LOOKS LIKE THEY'RE OUT SHOPPING.
THEY'RE DRINKING MILK?
WHY MILK?
GUESS IT'S OK.

FWOMP
これだわ!!
THAT'S IT!
Hey, Daidoji!
How to enjoy milk
Look up to the sky, place your hand on your hip.
And down it all in one gulp...
p-huh
BLEH
PASTEURIZED MILK THAT YOU BUY AT SUPERMARKETS HAS LITTLE NUTRITIONAL VALUE!!
M... MAYURA.

I WANT SPICA TO HAVE REAL MILK!!
DON'T BOTHER. IT'S TOO MUCH TROUBLE.
dab
dab
WAAAUGH
THIS IS MY LAST CHANCE TO MAKE FRIENDS WITH SPICA! LOKI, YOU MEANIE!
BWAAUGH
OH MAN. LOKI MADE A GIRL CRY AGAIN! HE'S THE WORST!
......

ARE YOU SURE THERE'S A RANCH...
...IN THE MIDDLE OF A FOREST LIKE THIS, MAYURA?
......
WE'VE BEEN WALKING FOR A WHILE...
THE SUN'S DOWN ALREADY. THOUGHT YOU WERE GONNA FEED US BARBECUE AT A RANCH...
I'M SURE OF IT. I WENT THERE ALL THE TIME ON MY WAY HOME.
I USED TO HAVE FRESH MILK EVERY DAY!
I JUST FORGOT HOW TO GET THERE...
WHEN DID YOU USED TO GO?

WHEN I WAS SIX OR SEVEN.
THAT'S WHY I HAVE SUCH A NICE BODY.
POSE!
I'M HUNGRY!
I HAVE A FEELING WE'LL NEVER GET THERE...
OH, WHAT'S THE MATTER, SPICA?
WHERE ARE YOU GOING?
AH!

SPICA?
I BET SHE SAW I WAS IN TROUBLE AND WENT TO THE HOUSE TO GET HELP.
A BUDDING FRIENDSHIP
LUCKY YOU!

LET'S FOLLOW HER!
I GUESS ...
HELLO!
ギャーッ
GAAUGH!
W-WHAT'S THE MATTER, YOU TWO?! WHERE'S SPICA?
YEAARGH! IT'S A COW!
モー
MOOOOO
オオ

Why on earth is a cow in the house...?
STEPHANIE IS OUR HOUSE COW.
IS THIS YOUR HOUSE? I THOUGHT THERE WAS A RANCH AROUND HERE.
HAVE YOU SEEN A GIRL IN A MAID'S UNIFORM?
WOW! GUESTS! WOULD YOU CARE TO JOIN ME FOR DINNER?
I'LL EAT, I'LL EAT!

SIMMER
SIMMER
SIMMER
WOW! IT'S ODEN!
ODEN...
Pass the mustard!
YOU LIVE HERE ALONE?
YES. THE CLEAN AIR HERE IS GOOD FOR MY POOR HEALTH.
THE DAUGHTER OF A RICH FAMILY, EATING ODEN ALONE...
I LIKE BARBECUE, BUT ODEN'S **DELICIOUS**! WHICH INGREDIENT DO YOU LIKE BEST, DAIDOJI?
THAT ONE!
munch
munch
BUT WHAT ABOUT THE RANCH?
I'M GLAD YOU TWO ARE ENJOYING THE FOOD, BUT...
WHAT ARE WE GOING TO DO ABOUT SPICA?

SPICA EATS LIKE A HORSE, BUT SHE HASN'T SHOWN UP.
WHAT HAPPENED?
HERE, LOKI.
A MOCHIKIN. ♡
TH... THANKS.
MUNCH
MUNCH
むぐむぐ
I GUESS WE SHOULD GO LOOK FOR HER...
むぐむぐ
MUNCH
MUNCH
TOTALLY STUNNED
茫然自失。
HUH? WHAT'S THE MATTER?
WHAAAT! WE'RE LEAVING ALREADY?

WELL, AT LEAST HAVE SOME TEA.
MOCHIKIN, MOCHIKIN
SHUT UP!
THAT'S RIGHT. WE'VE GOTTA LOOK FOR SPICA.
WE CAME HERE TO LOOK FOR HER.
WELL, WE FOUND A **COW**, SO WE MUST BE GETTING CLOSER TO THE RANCH.
I GOTTA ASK HER WHERE THE RANCH IS BEFORE WE LEAVE.
THAT DOESN'T MEAN THERE REALLY IS A RANCH.
THANK YOU FOR THE DINNER.
YOU CATCH ON QUICK, DON'T YOU, NARUKAMI?
CLAP
CLAP
mustard
WE'RE HAVING BARBECUE AFTER THIS, RIGHT?
YOU SHOULDN'T OVEREAT.
......
mustard

WHERE'S THE KITCHEN?
IT'S SO OLD AND DARK... AND SCARY.
I SHOULDN'T THINK LIKE THAT OR IT REALLY **WILL** BE SCARY.
HA HA
SPICA! SO YOU **ARE** HERE IN THE HOUSE.
HEY, SPICA!
SLAM
SPICA, LOKI IS WORRIED ABOUT YOU.
HUH? IT WON'T OPEN.
K-CHK
K-CHK
IS IT LOCKED?

AAAAAAAUGH!
WHAT HAPPENED, MAYURA?!
HFF
HFF
LOKI.
I FOUND SPICA. B... BUT...
I SAW AN EYE... THE KEY-HOLE...
YOU AREN'T MAKING ANY SENSE!

I SEE. SPICA IS HERE. MAYBE SHE'S LOST SOMEWHERE IN THIS BIG HOUSE.
SHE DOES GET LOST, EVEN IN MY HOUSE.
LET'S SPLIT UP AND LOOK FOR HER.
I'M SO SCARED! I DON'T WANT TO BE ALONE.
OKAY, THEN. MAYURA, YOU GO WITH NARUKAMI.
SEE YA LATER.
Waaaugh, Loki!!
WHAT, I'M NOT GOOD ENOUGH?
LOKI IS MORE DEPENDABLE.
NARUKAMI ONLY THINKS ABOUT HIMSELF.
HOW CAN YOU SAY SUCH A HORRIBLE THING SO CASUALLY?

OPENING THE DOOR WAS REALLY EASY.
K-CHK
ガーチャ

HOW STRANGE!
IS IT A STORAGE ROOM?
IT'S A STORAGE ROOM, BUT IT'S BIGGER THAN MY BEDROOM. NO FAIR.
BUB
BUB
THIS DRESSER WILL LOOK GREAT IN MY ROOM.
HEY, WHAT'RE YOU LOOKING AT?
NOBODY'S USING IT. THEY SHOULD LET ME HAVE IT.
HMM?
WHAT'S THIS PICTURE?
HUH? WHAT'S WRONG?

HEY, DAIDOJI. LOOK AT THE DATE!
IT'S TOO DARK, I CAN'T...
ゴロ
RUMBLE
RUMBLE
ゴロ
ゴロ...
FLASH
ば
FWSH
WHAT WAS THAT? THUNDER?
THP
THP
HUSH

NARUGAMI, THIS DATE IS...!
NO ONE IS HERE.
NO WAY!
HEY, SPICA!
WHERE DID YOU GO? I'M RIGHT HERE.
OH DEAR. MAYURA'S HUNT FOR MILK TURNED INTO A TOTAL BUMMER. I HOPE I CAN GO HOME TODAY.
!
THAT'S SPICA'S SHOPPING BASKET!

ギイ・・・
CREAK
バターン!
SLAM
HERE YOU ARE. I MADE SOME TEA...
BUT BY THE TIME IT WAS READY, EVERYONE WAS GONE.

S... SORRY. MY FRIEND SEEMS TO BE LOST IN THIS HOUSE.
I'LL BE LEAVING AS SOON AS I FIND HER.
PLEASE STAY...
GRAB

FWWSH
WHAT ARE
YOU ...?
SORRY, BUT I AM A GOD.
I KNOW YOU WANTED TO SUCK OUT A HUMAN SOUL.

YOU ARE
DEAD, RIGHT?
YES...
I AM.
SHE WAS POSSESSING SPICA'S BODY.
HERE YOU ARE, LOKI! TAKE A LOOK AT THIS PICTURE!

THIS IS THE LADY WHO SERVED ODEN TO US.
THIS PICTURE IS 50 YEARS OLD!!
THAT LADY... SHE **IS** A GHOST?!
HEY! WHAT'RE YOU DOING BREAKING INTO MY HOUSE?!
IT'S THE STORE MANAGER!
WHAT?
STORE MANAGER?
OH, IT'S NARUGAMI.
YEAH. HE MANAGES THE DAIRY I WORK AT.

UMM, WHAT ARE YOU DOING HERE?
THIS HOUSE'S BEEN VACANT FOR YEARS, BUT IT'S MINE.
THE SHOP IS BEHIND THIS HOUSE.
THE RANCH USED TO DO FINE, BUT BUSINESS HAS BEEN BAD.
YOU MEAN THE RANCH IS GONE?
GREAT! I CAN GO HOME!
WHERE DID YOU FIND THAT PICTURE?!
THAT'S MY AUNT. SHE WAS VERY PRETTY, BUT IN POOR HEALTH.
SHE DIED LONG BEFORE I WAS BORN.
Old lady.
BLRARGH...

SPICA CAN BE EASILY POSSESSED BY SPIRITS.
THEN SOMETHING LIKE THAT MAY HAPPEN AGAIN.
しゃこ brush
しゃこ brush
IS HE BEHIND THIS, TOO?
GOOD MORNIN'!!
BLEH
THAT'S MAYURA...
WHAT THE HECK IS SHE DOING UP SO EARLY?

I AM HERE TO DELIVER FRESH MILK FOR YOU, SPICA!
MILK ALWAYS TASTES BEST IN THE MORNING!
TEAR DROP
TEAR DROP MILK
POP
MILK
AH
GULP
GULP
GULP
GULP
YUMMY
I DID IT!
PFFF
TEAR DROP

ONE MORE, AS PROOF OF OUR FRIENDSHIP!
GULP
GULP
IT'S LIKE YOU'RE FEEDING PIGEONS, MAYURA.

CHAPTER 3
Pets are Family

FWEEE
VWOOO
......
ちら
GLANCE
IS IT JUST ME?
CHP
CHP
K-CHK
カチャ

HELLO!
MASTER LOKI!!
HI SKULD, LONG TIME NO SEE.
HELP YOURSELF TO SOME TEA.
THEY'RE HAVING A HAPPY GET-TOGETHER, AS IF NOTHING HAPPENED.
OH, MY. MASTER LOKI, ARE YOU ALL ALONE?
YEAH. EVERYONE WENT OUT SHOPPING FOR DINNER.
WHAT A NICE FAMILY LIFE YOU HAVE!

BY THE WAY, WHAT ARE YOU MAKING?
I FORGED IT BY MELTING DRAUPNIR, THE MAGICAL RING.
ITS NAME IS LAEVATEINN!
WHAT?! YOU MELTED DRAUPNIR?!
YEAH? DID I DO SOMETHING BAD?
SHUDDER
VERDANDI... VERDANDI...
SHUDDER SHUDDER
OH NO... I FORGOT ABOUT THAT. WHAT DO I DO NOW?

キィ
CREAK
AH!
OH, IT'S FENRIR, THE OLDEST SON OF MASTER LOKI.
A HUGE WOLF WHOSE JAWS REACH FROM THE HEAVENS TO THE EARTH.
GOOD MORNING, DADDY. WOOF WOOF.
PAT
OR THAT'S WHAT I HEARD...
HELLO, FENRIR! DID YOU HAVE A NICE NAP?

IT'S TIME FOR OUR WALK, DADDY!
ALREADY? I TOTALLY LOST TRACK OF THE TIME.
IT'S ALMOST COMPLETE, BUT EVERYONE IS OUT. WHAT SHALL I DO?
HERE!
ME! ME!
MASTER LOKI, I, SKULD, VOLUNTEER FOR THE MISSION!!
FWP FWP
HEY, SKULD...
LET'S GO, FENRIR! WE'RE GOING FOR A WALK-A-THON!!
THMP THMP
THMP THMP
YIP YIP.
WHAT DID YOU COME HERE FOR?
SKULD-
F.WOOOOO
HEY GIRLIE, WHY'RE WE WALKIN' IN SUCH A DESOLATE PLACE? IT'S BORING.

What an obnoxious dog!

Master Loki, forgive me. I came to take Fenrir back without letting Urd know.

If Fenrir is with you, Master Loki,

フェンリルさんとロキ様が一緒にいることでアレが……

THAT will happen sooner than it should.

アレが引き起こされるのが早まってしまうんです!!

Yes. It is also to protect you, Master Loki.

THEREFORE, FENRIR,

HUH?

DON'T PUT UP A FIGHT.
YEAAARH
ギャー
ギャー
YEAAARH
WAAUGH! WHAT'RE YOU DOING? YOU TRYING TO TIE ME UP AGAIN? I'M GONNA TELL MY DAD!
SHUT UP! I'M **NOT** ENJOYING THIS! ESPECIALLY SINCE IT'S SOMETHING MASTER LOKI WILL HATE ME FOR.
THMP THMP THMP
Classifieds
DON'T YOU REMEMBER YOUR BIG SISTER BROUGHT ME HERE?
WHY YOU TAKIN' ME **NOW**?
GRRR
SHE DOESN'T KNOW I'M HERE.
I'VE GOTTA DO THIS BEFORE THEY FIND US.
THD THD THD

To ordinary people, Fenrir's words sound ⬅ like this.
BOW WOW BOW WOW.
BOW WOW.
OUTPOURING
MELODY
BOW WOW
わわわんわーん
BOW WOW
わんわんわわーん
AH!
ビッ
BWHIP
WHUMP
びったーん
WAAAUGH!!
びー!!
HOW HUMILIATING! IT HURTS!
NRGH
うんしょ
FLUSTER
うんしょ
NRGH
GOOD. IT'S UNDONE!
I WON'T MISS THIS TIME, FENRIR.

FENRIR??
HOW'S THAT?
NOW TO TEST IF THE MAGIC OF THE RING WORKS IN THIS NEW FORM.
LOVELY SILHOUETTE.
Easy graduation
PRACTICAL USE.
TOTTER
ヨロ
ヨロ
TOTTER
When I have back pain
THIS WILL MAKE ME THE NEW MYTHICAL DETECTIVE LOKI.
A HA HA HA
MASTER LOKI-

WHAT? YOU LOST FENRIR?
FENRIR WAS SO CRUEL. WE WERE JUST PLAYING TAG, AND HE GOT SO SERIOUS.
SOB
SOB
I AM TOTALLY WORN OUT.
HE'S SO CUTE...
HUH?
MY BOY IS SO CUTE, SOMEONE MIGHT KIDNAP HIM!
A DOTING PARENT
IT'S TOO RISKY TO LEAVE HIM ALONE!
SHOCK

WE GOTTA GO LOOK FOR HIM. HE MAY BE TERRIFIED!
OR LOST SOME-WHERE!
OR PICKING UP FOOD OFF THE STREET!
GGGRAB
MASTER LOKI-
(OF COURSE) YOU'LL HELP ME, RIGHT, SKULD?
HM
OLD MAN'S WORRIES
DOWNSIZING IS NEAR.
BA-DUMP
WHY?
YES!
WHAT A FAMILY MAN... ♡
YAAY
LET ME TELL YOU HOW STRONG AND BRAVE I AM, NAGISA.
I BIT OFF THE ARM OF THE SO-CALLED BRAVEST GOD. ISN'T IT AMAZING?
HA HA HA
YOU LIKE MY STORY?

↑
Doesn't hesitate to commit random acts of cruelty.

BOW WEE WOW WOW WOW
I'LL TELL YOU MORE OF MY HEROIC STORIES.
THIS DOG REALLY SOUNDS LIKE HE'S SINGING. HE'S A DOG GENIUS!
NAGISA, WHAT ARE YOU DOING IN THE SHOP?
HI, DAD!
PUPPY CHOW
OIL
ARE'NT YOU GOING TO BE LATE FOR TUTORING?
I'M HELPING YOU BY CLEANING UP.
.....
DAMN. WE WERE JUST STARTING TO HAVE FUN.
MAN, IT'S THIS LATE ALREADY? I'VE STAYED HERE TOO LONG.
THE OLD MAN'S WAITING FOR ME.
SNACK TIME
BYE, NAGISA. SEE YA!
GRAB

KER-CHAK
SKULD, WHY WERE YOU WALKING IN SUCH A DESERTED NEIGHBOR-HOOD?
SHUDDER
I'M SO SORRY... MASTER LOKI.
FENRIR LIKES BUSY PLACES, LIKE SHOPPING MALLS.
PHEW!
WHAT'S THIS ROPE DOING HERE?
SHUDDER
SHUDDER

IT'S A KID-NAPPING!
HE GOT DOGNAPPED!
He's **NOT** accusing ME, but I feel very guilty.
WELL, WE DON'T KNOW IF HE WAS KIDNAPPED. LET'S KEEP LOOKING, MASTER LOKI.
I don't have time, either.
YOU'RE RIGHT.
HMMM
BY THE WAY, WHY DID YOU COME HERE, SKULD?
SHOCK

Uh-oh!
I thought
I distracted him,
but he is coming
straight at me!!
TO TAKE THE DOG FOR A WALK, OF COURSE.
I SEE. YOU MUST REALLY LIKE DOGS.
WELL...
OF COURSE NOT!
PKOW!
FWWP
Where did that coffee table come from?
NORNS NEVER TELL US THE IMPORTANT DETAILS.
GRRR
THAT'S BECAUSE WE NORNS ARE...
THE GODDESSES OF FATE.

ONCE DESTINY BEGINS TO UNFOLD, THERE IS NOTHING I CAN DO FOR YOU.
SKULD...
THOUGHT AT LEAST I COULD TAKE THE DOG FOR A WALK.♡
FENRIR!! THAT'S RIGHT! I WAS LOOKING FOR HIM.
HUH? THERE'S A PET SHOP.
PET SHOP
INAZUMA
IT DOESN'T LOOK BUSY AT ALL (NO PEOPLE AROUND).
They're going to sell Fenrir!
MGRR
MGRR
MASTER LOKI, CALM DOWN!

PET SHOP
INAZUMA
YES, OF COURSE.
A CONNOISSEUR LIKE CHAIRMAN YAMADA WOULD DEFINITELY APPRECIATE IT.
BARK
バウ
WHAT-CHA GONNA DO WITH ME, DAMN YOU??
LISTEN! I AM FENRIR, SON OF LOKI.
バウ
BARK
バウ
BARK
CAN YOU HEAR HIM SING?
HIYOKO
LISTEN TO ME!
BOOOW WOW WOW

THIS RARE DOG WILL BE SOLD TO A GOOD CUSTOMER...
CLICK
BEEP
BEEP
WHO...
YOU CAN'T SELL MY KID!
THERE WAS A KIDNAPPER! NO... DOG SNATCHER...??
DADDY!

GRAB
BWWSH
KID, ARE YOU THE OWNER?
JUST LET ME HAVE THIS DOG!
Daddy--
FENRIR!!

Daddy, I'm scared of knives!!
MASTER LOKI?
GRR
TREMBLE
ANGER
TREMBLE
ANGER
PING
ZING
RRROAR
FWSH

VGOOORR
KONK
GAAURGH!
HE'S FAMILY, SO FORGET IT.

WELCOME BACK, FENRIR. ♡
CATCH
That must hurt.
AAAH... IS HE ALRIGHT?
YUP. THAT WAS JUST A SHOCK FROM DRAUPNIR.
HE'S NOT ACTUALLY HURT.
F-WUP
Ah! You're right.
HEY. SKULD?
THUP
THUP
EXCUSE ME. COULD YOU PLEASE TELL ME...
HUH?
WHAT IS SO CUTE ABOUT THIS DOG?

I'M SORRY.
OUR BUSINESS IS SO TERRIBLE...
THE LOCATION IS NOT CONVENIENT FOR YOUR CUSTOMERS.
THERE'S NO ONE ON THE STREET!
I WOULD LIKE TO MOVE TO A BUSIER STREET, BUT I CAN'T EVEN AFFORD TO HIRE ANY HELP.
EH? YOU LIVE ALONE WITH YOUR DAUGHTER?
PET FOOD
PET FOOD
YOU'VE GOT NAGISA.
I CAN'T MAKE HER HELP ME. SHE'S JUST A CHILD.
YES
I DON'T THINK SO AT ALL!
DAD!

NAGISA!
I HEARD YOU.
I WANT TO HELP!
!
FWUP
WOULDN'T YOU RATHER PLAY WITH YOUR FRIENDS, NAGISA?
NOPE!
WE'RE FAMILY!

I WITNESSED HOW DECISIVE YOU CAN BE FOR THE FIRST TIME, MASTER LOKI.
OF COURSE! WE'RE FAMILY!
DADDY. ♡
LAEVATEINN WORKED GREAT.
SO DOES THIS MEAN YOU'RE WORKING ON STRENGTHENING YOUR MAGIC POWER, MASTER LOKI?
YEAH.

THIS MEANS YOU WISH TO RETURN TO THE WORLD OF THE GODS IN YOUR ORIGINAL FORM, RIGHT?
IF SO, WHY DID YOU REFUSE WHEN URD CAME TO GET YOU?!
I DIDN'T WANT TO BE UNDER THE CONTROL OF URD.
SHUDDER
ぎくぎくーッ
I BET NEITHER YOU NOR VERDANDI HAVE ANY IDEA WHAT URD IS THINKING.
I'D RATHER DO IT MYSELF.

I SEE.
I'M GOING TO HELP YOU, MASTER LOKI.
WHAT?!
WHAT?!
I WAS TAKING FENRIR FOR A WALK! I'M GOING BACK!
GRRR
NOOO—! I don't wanna go with HER!
SKULD, HAVE YOU GONE NUTS?!
MASTER LOKI!

FWMP すぽっ
STARE
じろ じろ
MASTER LOKI, WHO IS THIS GIRL?
PSSPSSPSS
ごにょごにょ
ACTUALLY ...
FLUSTERED
おろおろ
NO WAY...
CONFUSED
たじ...
IT CAN'T BE...
ZING
ぴゅーっ
NOOO!!
......

SO YOU'RE WALKING FENRIR.
SOMETHING LIKE THAT.
WELL, LET'S ALL OF US WALK AS A FAMILY.
TEN
TEN-AN

OH, THERE'S A DOG! HE'S SO CUTE.
MASTER LOKI HAS A DOG FETISH.
SHOCK
So it WASN'T a father's love for his son?!

My dear brother...
Come and help me...
I need you...

ODIN...
WHAT DO YOU WANT ME TO DO?
DIE.

GONK
OH, WHY ARE YOU...
ALWAYS LIKE THAT?
THUD
WHAT?!
WHAT THE...? IS THIS NARUKAMI'S...?
SPICA!

CHAPTER
The Cheerleading Club

SCHOOL HAS BEEN OUT FOR A WHILE. HE'S LATE.
OH!
WAVER
ふら
JUSTICE ...
THE WORLD ORDER ...
げっそり。
EXHAUSTED
WAVER
フラ
WAVER
フラ
HEY! NARU-KAMI!
FWUMP
コテ
HUSH
し――ん

IS HE DEAD?
POKE
POKE
OH, IT'S YOU, LOKI.
DON'T BEAT UP THE DEAD.
LOKI, I'M FINISHED. I'M NOT THOR ANY MORE, I'M JUST A HIGH SCHOOL KID. I'M NO GOOD AT KEEPING THE PEACE. I CAN'T EVEN KEEP ORDER IN SCHOOL.
ACTUALLY, YOU ALWAYS LOOKED LIKE A HIGH SCHOOL KID.
POKE
POKE
NOW THAT I LOST MY MYTHICAL MJOLLNIR, MY COMPANION THROUGHOUT COUNTLESS BATTLES, ALL THAT IS LEFT FOR ME IS TO FADE INTO OBLIVION.
YOU DIDN'T EAT DINNER LAST NIGHT, DID YOU?
POKE
POKE
HUH?!
シャキーン
ENERGIZED
BECOMING
Yaaay! It's my Mjollnir!
Is your wooden sword food to you?

YOU SEE, IF IT'S THAT IMPORTANT TO YOU, YOU WOULDN'T HAVE LOST IT.
STRAWBERRY MILK
THE JAPANESE CHARACTER FOR "BUSY" MEANS "LOSING ONE'S MIND."
I THINK IT'S WAY TOO BIG. MAKE IT SMALLER.
LIKE HOW?
I WOULD DO...
STRAWBERRY MILK
SOMETHING LIKE THIS?
PWOOF
ARE YOU KIDDING?
glance
glance
WHAT IS THAT, LOKI?

THIS IS LAEVATEINN.
IT'S A BEEFED-UP VERSION OF DRAUPNIR, THAT ABSORBS MAGICAL POWER.
SO YOU WANT THE KIND OF RELATIONSHIP I HAVE WITH MJOLLNIR?
WE **DO** LOOK PRETTY COOL TOGETHER.
WHO LOOKS COOL?
DO **NOT** COMPARE MY LAEVATEINN TO SOME ORDINARY WOODEN SWORD.
THIS NOBLE DESIGN AND **THAT** STICK? NO WAY.
カチン☆
ANNOYED
WHAT DID YOU SAY?! ARE YOU RIDICULING ME AND MY MJOLLNIR?
MAYBE I AM. BUT IT'S THE TRUTH.
KONK

AAOUCH!! WHAT THE HECK IS THIS?!
S... SORRY!
LOKI AND NARUGAMI!
WHAT ARE YOU DOING HERE, LOKI?
I CAME TO SEE NARUKAMI. ARE YOU IN SOME CLUB, MAYURA?
YUP. THE SOCCER CLUB WANTED ME TO HELP THEM.
BUT I HAVE AN IMPORTANT JOB AS MANAGER OF THE MYSTERY CLUB.
MUMBLE
WOW, I HAD NO IDEA YOU WERE A CHEERLEADER.
I THOUGHT YOU WERE THE ONLY MEMBER.

TWIRL
FWIP
CATCH
TEE HEE
THANKS FOR WATCHING!
WOW!! DAIDOJI, YOU ROCK! YOUR BATON MOVED LIKE IT WAS TOTALLY PART OF YOU.
IMPRESSED!!
WOW! I AM IMPRESSED! YOU SHOULD QUIT THE MYSTERY CLUB.

MAYURA, YOU **ARE** AMAZING! I COULD NEVER DO THAT.
I'M NOT IMPROVING AT ALL.
COME ON, TSUBASA! NO ONE **STARTS** GOOD. LET'S KEEP WORKING!
AFTER ALL, YOU BECAME A CHEERLEADER TO CHEER FOR YAMADA'S SOCCER GAMES.
I FEEL MY PASSION HEATING UP.
RRRRUMBLE
HUH?
LOKI!! LET'S HAVE A MATCH AND SEE WHICH ONE OF US HAS A STRONGER BOND WITH OUR PARTNER!
LET'S PRACTICE!
GRAB
YOU WIN. THAT'S FINE WITH ME. GET YOUR HAND OFF ME, PLEASE.
HEY, DAIDOJI!! LET US JOIN YOU!
SURE.
THIS MAN IS KIDNAPPING ME! **HELP**!

SMILE
I'D LOVE TO HAVE SOMEONE LIKE YOU WITH US.
I WANT TO DO CHEERLEADING WITH LOKI, TOO!
URGH.
It's not Loki's nature to decline a maiden's invitation.
FRANTIC
DAMN. WHY CAN'T I DO IT LIKE DAIDOJI?!
FRANTIC
I WISH I HAD A CHEERLEADER!
TWIRL
OOPS
OOPS
OOPS
KLUNK

ENOUGH! LOKI, NARUGAMI, DON'T LET GO OF YOUR STICKS!

I'M SORRY...

NOW, EVERYONE, LET'S PRACTICE AGAIN!

END OF PRACTICE!

THE CLUB MANAGER!

GOOD WORK, MAYURA. SORRY TO MAKE YOU TRAIN THE NEW MEMBERS.

FUN, ISN'T IT? BUT WHY ARE YOU PUTTING SO MUCH EFFORT INTO IT?

HEH HEH. WE HAVE REASONS.

LET'S CALL IT QUITS, TSUBASA.

I'M GOING TO PRACTICE MORE ALONE.

OKAY. LET'S GO HOME, LOKI. MAYBE YOU'VE GOT AN INTERESTING CASE.

OH BOY... (SORROW) MAYURA **HAS** TO QUIT THE MYSTERY CLUB.

YO, DAIDOJI. HOW CAN I TWIRL THIS THINGY?

DAMN-
TRASH
TUE FRI Burnab
WED Non-burna
THU Recycle
Please separate.
QUIT SWINGING YOUR SWORD ON THE STREET! IT'S DANGEROUS!
NARUKAMI IS A KLUTZ.
heh heh heh
くるん
TWIRL
I DID IT!!
GLARE
OKAY, LOKI!! IT'S TIME FOR A MATCH!!
I DON'T WANT TO. IT'LL MESS UP MY LAEVATEINN.
OH NO!!

MY STAFF'S GONE!
I BET IT GOT SWITCHED WHEN YOU DROPPED IT, LOKI.
IT GOT SWITCHED WITH TSUBASA'S BATON.
I'VE GOTTA HURRY BACK TO SCHOOL.
GO GET IT, AND WE'LL HAVE OUR MATCH, LOKI!!
LOKI IS BEHAVING LIKE A KID. IT'S SO UNLIKE HIM.
HUH?
MAGICAL GIRL LOKI.♪
TRA LA LA ☆
I mean, Magical BOY Loki.
I can't be bothered.
ZOOM

WHAT AN INTERESTING STAFF! IT'S NOT REALLY HEAVY OR LIGHT.
SOME KIND OF KID'S TOY, MAYBE? DOESN'T LOOK LIKE IT, THOUGH.
SNIFFLE
くすん
I CAN'T PRACTICE MY BATON MOVES WITH THIS.
I'VE GOTTA GET BETTER BEFORE THE SOCCER GAME.
SO GOOD TO SEE YOU. OH, ARE THOSE ITALIAN SHOES YOU'RE WEARING?
MY HUSBAND GOT THEM ON A TRIP.
KONK
コン
OOPS, EXCUSE...
THEY DON'T LOOK NICE ON YOU AT ALL. YOUR FASHION SENSE IS TERRIBLE.
So THAT'S what you're REALLY thinking, eh?
EEEEK
WHAT MADE ME SAY THAT?
!
BUMP
COME ON IN!
COME ON IN!

OUR PRICES ARE HIGH!
AND OUR STUFF IS OLD AND IT STINKS!!
HEY, YOU! WHAT THE HECK ARE YOU SAYING?!
THEY WERE JUST DELIVERED!
FWP
FWP
FWP
FWP
......
Maybe it's...
...

MISS BLOWFISH, WHEN I'M WITH YOU I AM HAPPY AS A CLAM IN THE MEDITERRANEAN.
PHEW
SINCE I MET YOU, MY LIFE IS AS BEAUTIFUL AS THE CARIBBEAN SEA.
BWOP
MISS BLOWFISH ...
AIYA!

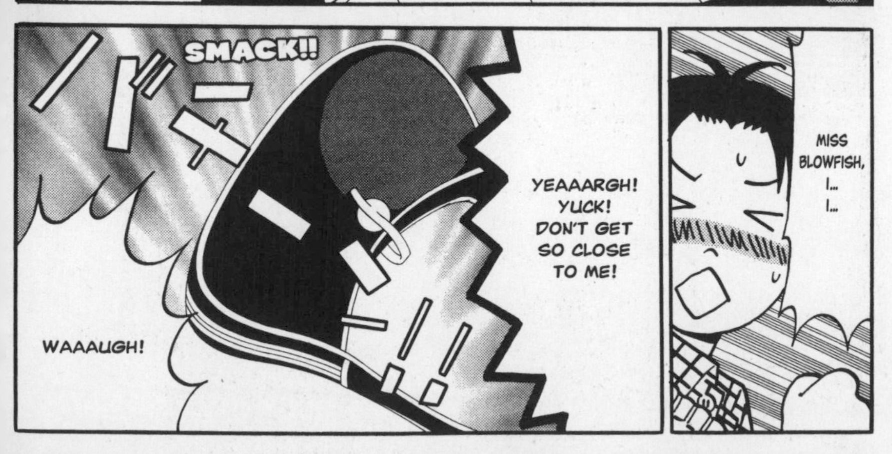
MISS BLOWFISH, I... I...
SMACK!!
YEAAARGH! YUCK! DON'T GET SO CLOSE TO ME!
WAAAUGH!

S...Sorry. Mr. Oyster, I didn't mean to...
I KNEW IT!
EVEN IF THIS IS A MAGIC STAFF, IT WON'T HELP ME WITH THE BATON.
Don't go, Mr. Oyster!
I'LL GIVE IT TO MAYURA TOMORROW.
DON'T GET SO UPSET OVER A TOY, LOKI. I'LL GET IT BACK TOMORROW.
SHOCK
HA HA HA HA HA HA
FEEL HOW LONELY IT IS WHEN YOUR PARTNER IS GONE.

I THOUGHT TSUBASA WAS IN THIS CLASS.
HI MAYURA!
OH, THE CHEERLEADING MANAGER. I'M LOOKING FOR TSUBASA.
I... I...
CALM DOWN, PLEASE!
I'M GONNA SEE YAMADA FROM THE SOCCER CLUB AFTER SCHOOL TODAY, AND TELL HIM THAT I LOVE HIM.
WHAT?
キャーーーッ ナイショー!!
YAAAY!! IT'S A SECRET!
An extremely excited little girl.
I think that's the same guy Tsubasa loves…
That's why she became a cheer-leader.
……

TSUBASA, DO YOU HAVE LOKI'S...
I've gotta change the subject!!
くる
WHIRL
TSUBASA?!
キーンコーンカーン
RRRRIING
GOOD TIMING. SCHOOL IS OVER.
THAT'S WHAT HAPPENED. I STILL CAN'T FIND IT.
どよーん
SHOCK
ARE YOU LISTENING TO ME, LOKI?
I THINK SO...

TSUBASA MUST BE UPSET. SHE'S KIND OF A LATE BLOOMER. I DON'T THINK SHE CAN COMPETE FOR YAMADA.
I'M AFRAID SHE'S OFF CRYING SOME-WHERE.
......
I'M GOING TO LOOK FOR TSUBASA.
ME, TOO.
LAEVATEINN'S MAGIC IS QUITE STRONG. I WONDER IF IT HAS SOME DIFFERENT EFFECTS WHEN A HUMAN USES IT.
ONCE SHE DISCOVERS IT, SHE WON'T BE ABLE TO RETURN IT. IT SEEMS LOGICAL. I'LL CHECK THE SCHOOL YARD.
Just as I expected. There's Tsubasa.
OH, LOKI!

WHEN I TRIED IT YESTERDAY, IT PROVED TO BE EFFECTIVE.
I HAVE TO MAKE SURE THE MANAGER WILL SAY, "I DON'T LIKE YOU, YAMADA."
BA-DUMP
BA-DUMP
YAMADA IS LATE.
HE'S ON CLEANING DUTY TODAY.
MY HEART IS ABOUT TO EXPLODE.
BA-DUMP
GRAB
I SEE. THAT'S THE EFFECT THE STAFF HAS.

IT'S NOT NICE TO MESS WITH PEOPLE'S HEARTS USING SOME TOOL.
LET'S SWITCH IT WITH THIS BATON.
NO!
WHY NOT? YOU CAN TELL HIM THAT YOU LOVE HIM YOURSELF.
HOW COULD I?! I'M NOT SURE OF MYSELF.
I'M SUCH A KLUTZ, AND I'M NOT GOOD AT ANYTHING, EVEN CHEERLEADING.
LOKI!
THMP
THMP
Narukami?!
THMP
THMP
I PRACTICED ALL NIGHT LONG! I CHALLENGE YOU!!

!
Monster!
EEEK!
FWP
IF YOU TRY REALLY HARD...
SWOOP
THERE'S NOTHING YOU CAN'T ACCOMPLISH!
GUARRRGH!

TWITCH
GUAAAAARGH
SCREAMS LIKE NARUGAMI
YEAAAARGH
HER HEART CAN'T HANDLE IT ANY MORE.
LOKI'S BEATING UP A GIRL... IT'S NOT LIKE HIM!
LIKE I SAID, IT'S DRAUPNIR'S MAGIC.
YOU SHOULDN'T LIMIT YOURSELF WHILE YOU'RE STILL YOUNG.
YOU SOUND LIKE AN OLD MAN.
HEY, SHOULDN'T YOU DO SOMETHING FOR THIS GIRL?
IF HER HEART IS AS CONNECTED WITH HER PARTNER AS OURS IS...
HER PARTNER WILL COME TO HER RESCUE!

HM...
GOOD, YOU'RE AWAKE. SOMEONE CALLED ME OUT HERE.
I GOT WORRIED WHEN I SAW YOU LYING ON THE GROUND.
YAMADA!
HERE'S YOUR BATON.
MAYBE YOU'RE ANEMIC. YOU'VE BEEN WORKING TOO HARD, PRACTICING EVERY DAY.
WHAT?
I'VE BEEN WATCHING YOU WORK HARD.
I'M COUNTING ON YOUR CHEERLEADING AT THE GAME!

I'M GLAD YOU GOT YOUR STAFF BACK.
LOKI!
I DON'T KNOW WHAT HAPPENED BETWEEN THE CAPTAIN AND YAMADA, BUT TSUBASA MIGHT QUIT CHEERING.
AND AFTER SHE WORKED SO HARD AT IT, TOO...
IF YOU FINALLY GET SOMETHING AFTER TRYING SO HARD,
YOU AREN'T GOING TO GIVE IT UP SO EASILY.
HEY LOKI!! SINCE YOU DEFAULTED, I'M THE WINNER.
DON'T GET CAUGHT UP IN WINNING OR LOSING.
GRR
WHY DIDN'T TSUBASA WANT TO GIVE THIS BACK TO LOKI?
WAS SHE USING IT AS A MASSAGE TOOL?
RUB
RUB
LIKE THIS

HEY, MAYURA. SHOW US THAT ROUTINE AGAIN.
YAMINO, WHAT'S FOR DINNER TONIGHT?
PORK SAUTÉ WITH GINGER.
HUH? THAT'S A HARD ONE.
YOU'RE LIKE MAYURA THE MAGICAL GIRL!
WOW–WE'RE HAVING MEAT!
TWIRL
TWIRL
TWIRL
SLIP
OOPS!
MEAT, MEA...
KONK
SORRY.
MEAT ...

I SHALL BE LEAVING NOW. THANK YOU VERY MUCH FOR YOUR HOSPITALITY.
BUT I DO NOT WISH TO IMPOSE ON OTHERS IN ANY WAY.
FWP
THUP
パタン...
K-CHK
He even closed the door quietly.
......
WHAAAT? WHAT HAPPENED TO NARUGAMI?
怖
SCARED
わた
FWP
わた
FWP
わた
FWP

DO THAT AGAIN TOMORROW, MAYURA.
HUH?
SMILE

Special Preview Comic

THE MYTHICAL DETECTIVE LOKI RAGNAROK

OH, DEAR. YOU SHOULDN'T HAVE SWEETS BEFORE BEDTIME. YOU'LL GET CAVITIES.
MUNCH
MUNCH
PLEASE MAKE SURE TO BRUSH YOUR TEETH BEFORE SLEEPING.
I KNOW, YAMINO.
DOZING
DOZING

NARUKAMI IS BEHIND THIS!
YEAAARGH- GAAURGH-
......
HE'S KILLING ME. JUST KILL ME!!
TREMBLE
WHAT THE HECK'S GOIN' ON, LOKI?!
I BROUGHT YOUR FAVORITE CRACKERS.
RICE CRACKERS
Baked with love and care
HE HAS BEEN CRYING IN PAIN ALL DAY.
I'LL TAKE THAT. THANK YOU.
WHAT'S WRONG?
MY TOOTH!!
YEOW
YEOW

TORNADO DENTAL
DENTAL CLINIC
BLUSH
I HEARD THE LADY DENTIST HERE IS BEAUTIFUL.
REALLY?
YEAARGH! NOOOO!
DRAG
DRAG
NEXT, COME IN, PLEASE.
I'LL GO IN WITH YOU.
K-CHK

OH MY, MASTER LOKI. COME IN, PLEASE. ♡
SLAM!
LET'S GO HOME, NARUKAMI. MY TOOTH IS BETTER.
WHAT?
GRAB
SO IS YOUR TOOTH HURTING? LET ME EXAMINE IT.
WHAT THE HECK ARE YOU DOING HERE, VERDANDI?!
YO, VERDANDI. YOU'RE WORKING IN THE HUMAN WORLD AS A DENTIST?
YEAARGH

MASTER LOKI, A CAVITY WILL NOT GO AWAY UNLESS YOU TREAT IT.
IF YOU WANT TO KEEP FEELING PAIN IN YOUR TOOTH, WE WON'T DO ANYTHING.
UGH
UUUGH
FLASH
Your bib, Master Loki.♥
Reya?!

Of all people,
why Verdandi?
I'm scared.
ZKSSHH
URGH
I could die!
THIS IS...!
WHAT?!
WHAT?
JUST A SIMPLE CAVITY.
AAH—
I TOLD YOU SO. WHAT WAS THAT SIGH FOR?!
YOU SHOULD GET AN EXPERT OPINION...
YEEAAUGH
DRILL
DRILL
IT HURTS!
IT HURTS!

NOD
NOD
DOES IT STILL HURT?
SOMETHING IS STRANGE! UNFORTUNATELY, I CAN'T USE MY POWERS.
GRR GRR
You can't?! But, I'm in pain!!
I CAN'T HELP BUT THINK THAT ODIN IS BEHIND THIS.
PAT
WHAT? REALLY?
WHAT?! ODIN IS RESPONSIBLE FOR MY CAVITY?
LOKI IS STUPID.
SPAT
LOKI IS STUPID.
SPAT
SOMETHING IS VERY STRANGE ABOUT THIS CAVITY.
SHWP SHWP
YAHOO
NO. MASTER ODIN IS POKING MASTER LOKI'S TOOTH WITH HIS SPEAR, GUNGNIR.

WE HAVE NO CHOICE. WE HAVE TO EXTRACT IT!
YAY! LET'S DO IT, DOCTOR! ♡♡
SOUNDS LIKE FUN! COUNT ME IN!
TA-DAA
The process of tooth extraction
Cut the gum with a scalpel.
↓
Open the gum with an elevatorium.
↓
Loosen tooth with an elevator.
↓
Pull out tooth with an extractor.
↓
Clean affected area with a scaler.
↑She went straight to this.
MAY I ASK YOU A QUESTION?
ARE YOU GOING TO USE ANESTHETIC?
ANESTHETIC? WE DON'T NEED THAT.
IF YOU'RE A MAN
GOLD TOOTH.

YEAAAAUGH

STOP IT! IDIOT!
HUFF
HUFF
FWUP
OOUCH ...
MAYBE I HAD THAT DREAM BECAUSE MY TOOTH HURT.
THROB
SOMEHOW IT SEEMS LIKE A PROPHECY.
THROB
THROB
It feels like something will happen.
ズキズキ
THROB
THROB
ズキ
THROB
I told you so.
Go see a dentist.
THE MYTHICAL DETECTIVE LOKI RAGNAROK 1 END

THE MYTHICAL DETECTIVE LOKI RAGNAROK VOLUME 1

Translator **EIKO McGREGOR**
Lead Translator/Translation Supervisor **JAVIER LOPEZ**
ADV Manga Translation Staff **KAY BERTRAND, JOSH COLE, AMY FORSYTH, BRENDAN FRAYNE, HARUKA KANEKO-SMITH AND MADOKA MOROE**

Print Production/ Art Studio Manager **LISA PUCKETT**
Pre-press Manager **KLYS REEDYK**
Art Production Manager **RYAN MASON**
Sr. Designer/Creative Manager **JORGE ALVARADO**
Graphic Designer/Group Leader **SCOTT SAVAGE**
Graphic Designer **CHY LING**
Graphic Artists **NATALIA MORALES, LISA RAPER, CHRIS LAPP AND NANAKO TSUKIHASHI**
Graphic Intern **MARK MEZA**

International Coordinator **TORU IWAKAMI**
International Coordinator **ATSUSHI KANBAYASHI**

Publishing Editor **SUSAN ITIN**
Assistant Editor **MARGARET SCHAROLD**
Editorial Assistant **VARSHA BHUCHAR**
Proofreaders **SHERIDAN JACOBS AND STEVEN REED**
Editorial Intern **JENNIFER VACCA**

Research/ Traffic Coordinator **MARSHA ARNOLD**

Executive VP, CFO, COO **KEVIN CORCORAN**

President, CEO & Publisher **JOHN LEDFORD**

Email: editor@adv-manga.com
www.adv-manga.com
www.advfilms.com

For sales and distribution inquiries please call **1.800.282.7202**

is a division of A.D. Vision, Inc.
10114 W. Sam Houston Parkway, Suite 200, Houston, Texas 77099

ISBN: 1-4139-0055-0
First printing, October 2004
10 9 8 7 6 5 4 3 2 1
Printed in Canada

The Mythical Detective LOKI Ragnarok Vol. One

PG. 10
Imagawayaki
A cylindrical Japanese sweet cake of red bean stuffed inside
a pancake-like batter. It is baked on a stove in an iron mold.

Okonomiyaki
A dish of pancake-like batter and vegetables (mostly cabbage) with a variety of meats and/or seafood. The whole ordeal is cooked on a hot plate and slathered with mayonnaise and special sauce.

Matsuo Basho's Haiku
"Summer grasses
all that remains
of soldiers dreams."

Kakkurakin
This was a popular TV show broadcasted in 1976 to 1986. The format was similar to *Saturday Night Live* and popular comedians performed in front of live audiences.

Oden
A winter dish of tofu, daikon, fish cakes, and other ingredients cooked in a special broth. Family and friends often eat from a large, communal pot called a *nabe* and eat with hot Japanese mustard.

Mochikin
Mochi (rice cake) inside fried tofu.

MYTHICAL DETECTIVE LOKI RAGNAROK

Detective work is tricky, but Loki is no stranger to the impossible! When the moon suddenly disappears, the search that ensues will unearth a surprising secret concerning Spica and her sleeping habits. Meanwhile, a silver-haired clone of Loki is walking the streets, looking to make a deal with the mythical detective, and it is somehow related to his sleeping sidekick. A slew of troubles weave a complex pattern, and it ll be up to the boy detective to solve yet another mystery in the tangled web of ***Mythical Detective LOKI Ragnarok*** **Volume 2.**